TEACHER

Inspiring Change One Child at a Time

I0151318

By: Orlando Worges

Email: nspireoasis@gmail.com

ISBN 978-1-0689781-0-4

eISBN 978-1-0689781-2-8

Cover Design and Cartoons: Orlando Worges

Acknowledgment

I am forever grateful for my parents' unwavering support and love throughout my journey as an educator. Their belief in the power of education has influenced my career and shaped my understanding of the profound impact teachers can have on their students' lives. It is with deepest gratitude that I acknowledge their guidance and encouragement.

Thanks to all the members of my family who were educators before me. Their dedication to the profession and commitment to shaping young minds has been a constant source of inspiration. I am grateful for the specific lessons they have taught me through their words and actions and for providing a strong foundation to build my journey as an educator.

A special thanks goes to my father, whose unwavering belief in education has driven my career. His encouragement and support have pushed me to pursue my passion and strive for excellence in everything I do. His guidance and wisdom continue to inspire me every day.

I am incredibly lucky to have a wife, family, friends, and colleagues who have stood by my side and supported me throughout my journey as an educator. Their unwavering belief in my abilities and their constant encouragement has been invaluable. Their strength and love have carried me through the challenges and triumphs of this profession; I am eternally grateful.

Foreword

As I reflect on my journey as an educator, I am reminded of my rich lineage. I am a fourth-generation teacher, following in the footsteps of my grandmother, mother, and older sister. I can still vividly recall the pride I felt as they sat there, attentively listening to my principal's address at my graduation. In that moment, three generations of teachers were symbolically united, and it was a testament to the profound impact teaching has had on our family.

Growing up, I had the privilege of closely observing the teaching practice – through my own experiences and watching others. I cannot deny a teacher's profound influence on a student's life. There were days when teachers were like idols, revered and respected. Their words held a weight that parents could not challenge, even when it concerned their children. Teaching was not merely a profession but a calling, a noble mission that went beyond a mere pay cheque.

But where are we now? The landscape of education has transformed, presenting its own set of challenges. Teaching is no longer viewed with the same level of esteem it once enjoyed. The profession has come under scrutiny, parental involvement has shifted, and new teaching methods and technologies have reshaped how we educate.

Yet, amidst the changes, we must never lose sight of our purpose as teachers. We must never forget the impact we can have, our reach, and the mission that binds us together: to positively change the world one child at a time. Despite the complexities and demands of modern education, we must remain unwavering in our commitment to our students and the communities we serve.

In the pages of "Teacher," we embark on a journey that explores the evolving landscape of education. Through stories, insights, and practical advice, we uncover the timeless principles, and the innovative approaches needed to navigate the challenges we face as teachers today.

Let this book be a source of inspiration, a reminder of our power, and a guide for aspiring teacher leaders. Together, let us rise to the occasion, reignite the love for teaching within us, and reignite the fire of passion and purpose that first led us into this remarkable profession. Our influence stretches far beyond the classroom walls – it has the potential to shape the future and transform the lives of generations to come.

Table of Contents

Foreword..*2*

The Power of the Teacher's Impact................................. *6*

1: You Always Have a Choice *10*

2: Believing in Something *12*

3: Love, Respect, Empathy, and Integrity: Key Attributes

for Educators... *17*

4: They Have Voices Too, Will You Listen?........................ *26*

5: We are Advocates *30*

6: Revelations of Redemption: A Journey from Despair to

Triumph.. *34*

7: The Power of Connection: A Teacher's Journey from

Detachment to Transformation.. *39*

8: From Devastation to Unity: Leading Through Tragedy 45

9: Beyond the Classroom *48*

10: Student Discipline Redefined *56*

11: Parallel Realities *61*

12: Look, Listen, the Signs are Always There... .... *63*

13: The Vision: The Transformed School........................... *68*

14: Unseen Potential: A Tale of Redemption *72*

15: Teacher Quality Matters..................................... *76*

The Power of the Teacher's Impact

Yes, I love teachers, and I love the profession. After all, I became a teacher myself," I mused, reminiscing about the journey that had led me to where I am today. Teaching, to me, was not just a job but a calling. It is a profession that holds immense power and responsibility, for the

choices we make and the impact of what we do could shape the lives of countless individuals. Our profession mattered, for we were the cornerstone of all other professions. These architects laid the foundation for the doctors, the lawyers, the police officers, the nurses, and even the thieves and murderers. We held the clay in our hands, molding and sculpting it into something meaningful that would carry a lasting impact.

As I sit here now, pen in hand, I find myself contemplating the questions at our profession's heart. Who passes through our classrooms daily? Who entrusts us with their precious minds and hearts? Are we truly aware of the immense responsibility placed upon our shoulders? And most importantly, what direction do we teach them to go?

In this book, my intention is not to cast judgment or assign blame. No, my purpose is far greater than that. It is a call for self-reflection, for teachers to pause and honestly examine our practices. To ask ourselves, "Did I do it right?" We must ponder the moments we may have missed and the opportunities we let slip through our fingers.

This is not just a call to teachers. No, I implore parents to read these words with an open mind and heart, to question themselves, "Did I listen and pay attention?" A child's education is not the sole responsibility of a teacher; it is a partnership that requires collaboration, understanding, and a shared commitment to the welfare and growth of our young minds.

But this book is not just for teachers and parents. It is also for students, for those who have sat in those very classrooms and allowed their minds to absorb the lessons, both academic and otherwise. I encourage you to read these pages not as a critique of your teachers or education, but as an opportunity to heal, reflect upon your experiences, and understand their profound impact on shaping your present self.

Let us remember the administrators and policymakers who have the power to shape the very systems in which we operate. I pray you, dear readers, pay attention and listen to the stories and experiences shared within these pages. By understanding the challenges and triumphs of those on the front line, we can make informed decisions that nurture and support the growth of our educational institutions.

So, what will you do after you have read this book? Will you close its covers and move on with your life, unchanged and unaffected? Or will you allow the words to seep into your soul, to challenge your beliefs and ignite a fire within you? Will you emerge a better version of yourself from this book, armed with the knowledge and awareness to effect positive change within your spheres of influence?

As I write these words, I am reminded of the countless teachers who have impacted my life. The ones who saw beyond my shortcomings and nurtured my potential. The ones who believed in me when I stopped believing in myself. These teachers inspired me to embark on this journey—to become a voice for those who may not have the courage or the platform to speak for themselves.

In the chapters, I will share stories and reflections woven together with research and insights garnered over years of experience. I intend not to impart a definitive roadmap or a step-by-step guide, for teaching is a deeply personal endeavor that requires adaptability and intuition. Instead, I hope to ignite a spark within you, to reignite the passion and purpose that led you to become a teacher in the first place.

So, let us embark on this journey together, dear reader. Let us embrace the power and potential of our profession. Let us listen, learn, and grow as we strive to create environments that foster curiosity, empathy, and critical thinking. In doing so, we honor ourselves and the young minds passing through our classrooms. They have voices, too. Will you listen?

1: You Always Have a Choice

The sun was beginning to rise over the horizon, casting its warm golden light across the vast expanse of the countryside. I had been walking for hours and was almost to my destination. I had been walking to school since I was old enough to go, and I had grown accustomed to the long journey. I had always preferred the walk, though. It was a peaceful time to think and reflect.

Today, however, my journey was interrupted. As I rounded a bend in the road, I felt something give way beneath my feet. I stopped and looked down, only to find that the sole of one of my shoes had come ultimately off. I had been wearing this pair for months and knew it was beyond repair. Going home was not an option, as I had already come too far. I had no choice but to continue, so I did the only thing I could think of. I grabbed a few elastic bands from my pocket and used them to hold the sole back onto the shoe. It was a makeshift solution, but it would have to do.

I continued on my way, my feet aching with every step. But I knew that I had to keep going. My parents had always taught me that education was my ticket to success, and I was determined to attend school. I had worked too hard to give up now.

The sun was high in the sky when I reached the school gates. I was exhausted, and my feet were sore, but I was relieved to have made it. I was greeted by a few of my classmates, who had already arrived. They were confused to see me arrive with my makeshift shoes, but I just shrugged it off and went inside. I spent the day at school and waited for my parents to get me another. Getting an education was just too important to let trivial things stand in the way.

W e had to attend church every Sunday after that weekly 5:00 a.m. family prayer meeting. My parents were firm believers in the power of prayer and ensured that we all prayed together at least once weekly. They believed that if we prayed, God would give us the strength and courage to face the day.

Although he barely made it to the ninth grade, my father

also firmly believed in the importance of education. He was determined that we would all get a good education, no matter what. He always encouraged us to study hard and do our best in school. He often said, "To be successful in life, you must get a good education. It's the only way to get ahead in life."

My father was also very strict about our education. He often told us, "If you don't take your education seriously, you won't be successful in life." He always pushed us to do our best in school and often rewarded us for getting good grades.

One day, I had no classes and decided to stay home. My father gave me my regular lunch money and said, "Take your education seriously; go to the library and read a book." His suggestion surprised me, but I knew he meant what he said. I grabbed my lunch money and headed to the library. I spent the day reading books and learning new things. I was amazed at how much I could learn from just one book. I was so inspired that I started writing my own stories and poems.

My father's words of encouragement and belief in the power of education profoundly affected my life. I graduated from college and university and enjoyed many successes in my career. I always remembered his words, "Take your education seriously, and you will be successful in life." My parents' belief in God and education helped shape me into who I am today. I am thankful for their support and guidance throughout my life. They taught me that I could achieve anything with hard work and dedication.

I was raised in a small town surrounded by rolling hills and lush forests, where the church was central to shaping my upbringing. The church was more than just a place of worship; it was where I learned invaluable life lessons that would stay with me forever. Sunday school was like a second home to me, a place where stories of courage, compassion, and kindness were woven into the fabric of my being. As a young boy, I soaked up the lessons of forgiveness shared with us. I learned that holding onto grudges only burdened the soul while letting go freed me to embrace peace and joy. Forgiveness became a cornerstone of my character, a guiding principle that helped me navigate the complexities of human relationships.

Vacation Bible School was a highlight of my summers, filled with songs, crafts, and vibrant lessons that brought the stories of faith to life in vivid colors. During one such VBS, I learned the importance of teamwork and collaboration. Working on group projects with my peers taught me that we could achieve great things by coming together with a shared goal. This lesson on teamwork became a valuable skill that I carried with me into adulthood, helping me build strong relationships and foster unity in my community.

Summer camps and retreats were cherished experiences that allowed me to escape the busyness of daily life and immerse myself in nature and spirituality. At camp, I discovered the power of solitude and reflection, connecting with myself and the world around me. The quiet moments spent by the campfire, gazing at the stars, provided a space for me to contemplate life's mysteries and find solace in the beauty of nature. One summer retreat left an indelible mark on my heart. The theme was resilience, and the speakers shared inspiring stories of overcoming adversity and finding strength in challenging times. Listening to tales of courage and perseverance made me realize that life was not always smooth sailing; there would be storms and trials along the way. But how I weathered those storms would shape my character and define my destiny.

Through all these experiences, Sunday school, Vacation Bible School, summer camps, and retreats. I understood that the church was a source of wisdom and guidance that extended far beyond its walls. The invaluable lessons I learned became the foundation upon which I built my life, serving as a compass in moments of uncertainty and an inspiration to be a beacon of light in a sometimes dark and challenging world.

As I ventured out into the world, the lessons I had gleaned from my church experiences remained with me, guiding me through life's twists and turns. In times of hardship, I drew upon the well of strength and resilience I had cultivated in those early years. When faced with difficult decisions, I turned to the principles of forgiveness and compassion that had taken root in my heart. And when I felt lost or alone, I sought solace in the beauty of nature and the comfort of community, knowing that I was never truly on my own.

Looking back on my journey, I realized that the invaluable lesson I had learned from going to church was that faith was not merely a set of beliefs to adhere to but a way of living and being in the world. It was about embodying kindness and compassion, nurturing resilience and strength, and finding joy and beauty amidst life's trials. Church had taught me that the principles and life skills I had cultivated were timeless truths that would accompany me on my lifelong journey. Wherever you teach, at school, church, a court, on a field on land or sea, what is your effect?

3: Love, Respect, Empathy, and Integrity: Key Attributes for Educators

Love

The sun was starting to rise, casting a warm glow over the quiet streets as I made my way to the school. The halls were still peaceful, but soon, they would be filled with the buzzing energy of students eager to learn. As I entered my classroom, I took a moment to breathe in the familiar scent of chalk and books. The anticipation of a new day washed over me, filling me with purpose and excitement. Early in my career as an educator, I first realized the power of love in the classroom. I had always believed in the importance of creating a nurturing and supportive environment, but one student truly opened my eyes to the transformative potential of love.

I'll never forget Lily, a bright-eyed, spirited ten-year-old who recently transferred to our school. She had a chaotic home life, navigating through parental divorce and a constant sense of instability. Lily's rebellious attitude and disruptive behavior became her defense mechanism, a way to hide her vulnerability and pain. In those early days, it would have been easy to dismiss Lily as a troublemaker, to label her as a lost cause. But something deep within me told me there was more to her story: underneath the tough exterior, there was a hurting soul in desperate need of love and understanding.

I made a deliberate choice to approach Lily with compassion and empathy. Instead of reprimanding her for her disruptive behavior, I pulled her aside one day after class and asked, "Are you okay?" Tears welled in her eyes as she began to share her story – a story of fractures and brokenness that no child should ever have to carry. From that moment on, I made it my mission to shower Lily with fatherly love. I greeted her with a smile every morning, asked her about her interests, and encouraged her to express herself through art and writing. I created a safe space where she felt seen and valued, where her voice mattered.

Slowly but surely, I witnessed a remarkable transformation. Lily's rebelliousness began to fade, replaced by a newfound curiosity and love for learning. She started to open up in class, voicing her thoughts and ideas with a newfound confidence. The once broken child had blossomed into a radiant young girl, capable of healing and growth. Lily's journey taught me that love was not merely a sentiment but a powerful force that could break through even the most formidable barriers. The anchor connected our classroom, fostering a sense of belonging and acceptance that allowed every student to thrive. Love became my guiding principle as an educator – a constant reminder of our profound impact on our students' lives.

Respect

Respect is a simple word that holds immeasurable power. As an educator, I quickly learned that respect was the cornerstone of an inclusive and empowering classroom. The thread wove together a diverse group of students, creating a tapestry of trust and mutual understanding. In our classroom, respect was not merely a set of rules to be followed but a way of being. We celebrated our differences, recognizing the unique perspectives and experiences that each student brought to the table. We listened to one another without judgment, genuinely hearing and honoring each voice.

However, respect went beyond student interactions – it extended to the relationship between teacher and student. I consciously tried to treat every student with dignity and kindness, acknowledging their strengths and challenges. I encouraged their autonomy, empowering them to take ownership of their learning. One student who embodied the power of respect was Daniel, a soft-spoken and introverted boy who seemed to fade into the background. Daniel had always struggled academically, often overshadowed by his more outgoing peers. But instead of dismissing him, I sought to understand the reasons behind his struggles.

Through open conversations and a sincere desire to connect, I discovered that Daniel had a hidden talent for visual arts. I encouraged him to express himself through his drawings and paintings, allowing him to shine in a realm where he felt honestly heard and seen. The respect I showed Daniel went beyond acknowledging his talent; it was about honoring his individuality and allowing him to define his path. I tailored my teaching strategies to meet his unique needs and gave him the support and encouragement he needed to flourish.

In time, Daniel's confidence began to soar. With each stroke of the brush, he found his voice, expressing emotions and ideas that had once been trapped within him. Through the power of respect, Daniel discovered his passion and found a sense of purpose in the classroom. Daniel's journey taught me that respect was not just a surface-level courtesy but a profound recognition of every student's inherent worth and potential. It was a commitment to creating an environment where students felt valued and respected, regardless of their background or abilities. Respect became the foundation upon which our classroom community thrived.

Empathy

Empathy is the ability to understand and share another person's feelings. Reflecting on my years as an educator, I realize that empathy is one of the most vital attributes we can possess as teachers. It is the key that unlocks the door to each student's world, allowing us to connect on a human level.

Every student who walks through our classroom doors comes with a unique set of experiences and challenges. For some, school is a sanctuary, a place of stability and support. For others, it is a battleground, an arena where they face prejudices, abandonment, and a sense of hopelessness. It was during my second year of teaching that I encountered Allison, a quiet and withdrawn fourteen-year-old who had recently lost her mother to cancer. The grief that weighed upon her was palpable, enveloping her in an invisible cloak of sorrow. She struggled to concentrate, to find joy in learning, and to navigate the complexities of adolescence.

Instead of dismissing Allison as a disengaged student, I chose a different path. I sought to understand her grief, to empathize with the emotions she carried within. I dedicated time every week to meet with her one-on-one, providing a safe space where she could share her thoughts, fears, and pain. Through our conversations, I realized that school had become an overwhelming reminder of the life she had lost. She felt disconnected from her peers and misunderstood by her teachers. It was clear that she needed more than just academic support;

she needed someone to acknowledge, validate, and understand the depths of her grief.

Incorporating empathy into my teaching practice, I worked closely with Allison to create a personalized learning plan that allowed her to heal while simultaneously pursuing her academic goals. By providing her with flexibility and understanding, we were able to navigate her grief together, ensuring she never felt alone in her journey. Over time, I witnessed a flicker of light return to Allison's eyes. Her weight began to lessen, and her enthusiasm for learning reignited. It was through empathy that I was able to support her in not just her academic journey but her emotional healing as well.

Allison's story taught me that empathy was a nice-to-have quality and an essential tool for effective teaching. It allowed me to truly see and understand my students, meeting them where they were and providing support tailored to their unique needs. Empathy became the bridge that connected our hearts and minds, fostering a deep sense of belonging and growth within the classroom.

Integrity

Integrity is the unwavering commitment to doing what is right, even when difficult. As educators, we are entrusted with a sacred duty—to mold and nurture young minds, guide them on a growth path, and instill the values that will shape their futures. However, integrity in education goes beyond teaching academic content; it encompasses modeling the principles and values we hope to instill in our students. It is about leading by example and fostering a classroom culture of honesty, fairness, and ethical behavior.

As an educator, I recognized my immense responsibility in shaping my students' future. I knew my words and actions would have a lasting impact beyond the classroom walls. My duty was to be a role model and demonstrate integrity in every interaction and decision. One incident stands out in my memory, a moment that tested my integrity and challenged the foundations of our classroom community. During an end-of-year exam, I noticed several students whispering and exchanging notes. The urge to ignore their actions and allow them to cheat washed over me like a tidal wave. After all, it was just one exam, and the pressure to succeed had engulfed them.

But something deep within me urged me to choose integrity. I knew that allowing dishonesty to go unchecked would compromise the trust and respect we had built in our classroom. It would convey that shortcuts and dishonesty were acceptable in pursuing success. With a heavy heart, I approached the students involved and addressed the cheating incident head-on. Instead of punishing them, I engaged them in a conversation about the importance of honesty and the long-term consequences of their actions. I offered them another chance, an opportunity to rebuild their integrity.

The incident became a catalyst for growth and reflection in the following days. We delved deep into discussions about integrity, examining real-life examples and exploring its impact on personal and professional success. It became a turning point, a moment that shaped the values of our classroom community. Through that experience, I witnessed the transformative power of integrity. It strengthened the bond between teacher and student, fostering a culture of trust and responsibility. It taught my students that success is measured not only by grades and accolades but also by the choices we make and the integrity with which we navigate our lives.

Integrity became the compass that guided our classroom, ensuring that every decision and action aligned with our shared values. It instilled the conviction always to choose what is right, even if it is the more difficult path. As a result, our classroom became a space where integrity thrived, providing a solid foundation for students to build their futures.

The resolve is that love, respect, empathy, and integrity are the cornerstones of effective education. They are the attributes that elevate teaching from a mere profession to a lifelong vocation. In a world where our students face countless challenges and obstacles, our educators must equip them with academic knowledge and the values that will guide them toward lifelong growth and fulfillment.

Love reminds us of our profound impact on our students' lives. It drives us to create a nurturing and supportive environment where every student feels valued and seen. Respect fosters an inclusive and empowering community where diversity is celebrated, and every voice is heard. Empathy connects us to the humanity of our students, allowing us to understand and support them on a deep and meaningful level. Integrity shapes the values and principles of our classroom, ensuring that our actions align with our words and our commitment to ethical behavior.

As educators, we must embrace these attributes, grounding our practice in love, respect, empathy, and integrity. By doing so, we can create classrooms that are not just centers of academic learning but also hubs of personal growth, where students are empowered to become compassionate, responsible, and resilient individuals. Reflecting on my journey as an educator, I am reminded of the young girl whose pain shattered my naivety and ignited a fire within. Her story fueled my relentless pursuit of change, propelling me to advocate for a system that prioritizes love, respect, empathy, and integrity.

For her and all the students who have shared their stories with me, I will continue striving for an education system that better serves their needs. Ultimately, our students inspire us and challenge us to be the best educators and human beings we can be. Their futures depend on our unwavering commitment to love, respect, empathy, and integrity.

4: They Have Voices Too, Will You Listen?

As the principal of Saint Mary's High School, I pride myself on being fair and just when it came to disciplinary action. So, when I received the letter recommending the suspension and possible exclusion of one of my students, I knew I had to investigate further. Sitting at my desk, I carefully read the report the teacher and the dean of discipline had submitted. Every detail was documented, painting a picture of a student who was grossly disruptive and

disrespectful in class. Although the evidence seemed stacked against her, I couldn't help but feel an urge to hear her side of the story.

Leaving my desk, I went to where the student, Sophia, and her mother were waiting. But as I arrived, I noticed Mrs. Martinez, Sophia's mother, heading towards the school doors, her eyes filled with shock and confusion. "Mrs. Martinez!" I called out urgently, my voice echoing through the hallway. "Please, wait! There has been a misunderstanding."

She turned around, her face etched with worry and frustration. "I was told I couldn't talk to you. They said you weren't present on the campus. How is that possible?" I hurriedly explained that there must have been a miscommunication and assured Mrs. Martinez that I was indeed the principal and that I had come to listen to her daughter's side of the story. Relief washed over her face as we made our way to an empty classroom where we could speak privately.

Sitting across from Sophia and her mother, I could see their fear and uncertainty of what lay ahead. I reassured them that I was there to listen, seek the truth, and ensure justice prevailed. As Sophia recounted her version of events, tears streamed down her cheeks. She explained that on that fateful day, she had asked the teacher, Ms. Johnson, for permission to use the bathroom as she felt unwell. However, Ms. Johnson had denied her request, insisting that she wait until after class. Sophia, desperate to relieve her discomfort, returned to her seat, hoping she could hold it in a little longer.

But fate had other plans. A few minutes later, overcome by a sudden wave of nausea, Sophia rushed back to Ms. Johnson, begging for mercy. It was too late. With no time to make it to the bathroom, Sophia vomited on the classroom floor, leaving an awful mess in its wake. In that moment of humiliation, Sophia was stunned to hear Ms. Johnson's callous words: "Look at what you caused. You are so disgusting; you sick a John Crow's stomach."

My blood boiled at the thought of a teacher stooping so low, demeaning a student already in distress. It was clear to me now that the disciplinary action taken against Sophia was unwarranted and deeply unjust. Determined to get to the bottom of the matter, I gathered statements from other students who had been present in the classroom that day. Their accounts further corroborated Sophia's story, painting a picture of a teacher who had neglected her duty of care and misbehaved towards a vulnerable student.

Armed with this overwhelming evidence, I called for an emergency meeting with Ms. Johnson, the dean of discipline, and the teacher's union representative. It was crucial to allow Ms. Johnson to respond and tell her side of the story, but the weight of proof against her seemed impossible. During the meeting, Ms. Johnson appeared defensive, her voice trembling as she tried to explain away her actions. She claimed that she had been stressed and overworked and lost her temper in the heat of the moment.

But no number of excuses could justify her treatment of Sophia. Clearly, her behavior was unprofessional and a breach of our school's code of conduct. After carefully considering all the evidence and hearing both sides of the story, the decision was clear. Ms. Johnson would face disciplinary action for the disparaging remarks and disregarding the well-being and dignity of a student under her care.

"They have voices too; will you listen?" became another mantra that resonated with us, reminding us of the power and importance of hearing the stories and experiences of those who often go unnoticed or dismissed. From that day forward, I vowed to listen genuinely to the words spoken and the unspoken fears and desires within each student. Their voices are the key to unlocking a future filled with compassion, justice, and understanding.

I decided to address the issue immediately. I took a deep breath and reassured the students that this classroom was a safe space where their voices and opinions mattered. I emphasized that making mistakes was an inevitable part of the learning process and that they should never feel embarrassed or afraid to speak up.

Slowly, the atmosphere began to shift. The students started to open up tentatively, but eventually, their hesitations melted away. They would share their thoughts and engage in discussions, contributing to the growth of everyone present. The classroom became a vibrant hub of curiosity and discovery.

Days turned into weeks and weeks into months. The bond between my students and I deepened, and I realized that my role as a teacher extended far beyond imparting knowledge. I became a mentor, a friend, someone my students could rely on during their education and personal growth journey. It was a responsibility that I cherished deeply.

One rainy afternoon, I received a phone call from a former student, Lily. She sounded distressed, and I immediately sensed that something was wrong. She confided in me about a teacher at her new school who constantly belittled and ridiculed her in front of her classmates. The teacher's biting words had shattered her confidence and made her dread going to school every day.

Stifling my anger at the teacher's behavior, I assured Lily I would do everything possible to help her. I contacted the school administration, documenting Lily's experiences and urging them to act. I couldn't bear the thought of another student enduring the same treatment that Lily had undergone, and days of back-and-forth discussions and meetings ensued, with the administration initially hesitant to acknowledge the seriousness of the situation. But I persisted, providing them with concrete evidence and testimonials from other students who had witnessed Lily's mistreatment. Eventually, the school began investigating, and the teacher was suspended pending further inquiry.

During this time, I had become Lily's advocate and a fierce protector for all my students. Aware of the potential retaliation they might face from their peers, I organized support groups for those who had witnessed or experienced mistreatment at the hands of educators. We created an environment where students could heal, speak out, and find solace in one another's stories.

As the investigation continued, more students stepped forward, sharing their experiences with teachers who used their power to hurt rather than educate. The issue was no longer limited to a single teacher but had uncovered a deeply rooted problem within the school system. My resolve to fight for change only grew stronger. In collaboration with parents, students, and fellow teachers who shared my vision, we formed a task force dedicated to addressing issues of mistreatment and promoting a nurturing environment for all learners. We organized workshops for teachers to understand the impact of their words and actions, encouraging empathy and compassion.

Over time, our efforts began to bear fruit. The school administration implemented new policies to prevent mistreatment and established anonymous reporting systems for students to voice their concerns safely. Teachers underwent extensive training on how to create inclusive, respectful classrooms. The fight for change was not without its challenges, but the transformation within the school was remarkable. Students felt freer to express themselves, to take risks, and to explore the world of knowledge boldly. As teachers, we became not just disseminators of information but cultivators of growth, empowering our students to thrive academically and emotionally.

Reflecting on my journey, I realized that every teacher has the power to shape lives. Every interaction and every word spoken within a classroom had the potential to mold not only minds but also hearts. In a world where good and evil coexist, I wanted to be the teacher who empowered, uplifted, and championed every student who walked through my door. I would continue to fight for change, challenge the norms that perpetuated harmful practices in education, and ensure that the classrooms of tomorrow were filled with compassion, respect, and the freedom to learn, explore, and grow.

6: Revelations of Redemption: A Journey from Despair to Triumph

The pain etched on her young face was evident as tears streamed down her cheeks, leaving trails of devastation in their wake. The weight of her secret burden defined her, transforming her from an innocent eighth grader into a shell of her former self. She had never planned for this to happen; it was unexpected, uncontrollable. With a trembling hand, she whispered, "How could he not have seen it? The first time it happened, I sent him a text message expressing my fear."

It was an inconceivable truth that she carried – a truth that shattered the foundation of her life. Sundays were spent in their church's comforting embrace, basking in their faith's love and guidance. Being sexually active was never a part of the plan, yet it had become her reality. She knew better. She should have done better. But now, as she sat with her heart in tatters, she feared her father's reaction. "Daddy is going to kill me," she whispered, trembling with guilt.

Going home was no longer a safe sanctuary for her fragile soul. Though she knew she was the apple of her father's eye, the thought of facing him and revealing her darkest secret felt insurmountable. With dread-filled hours dragging by, they awaited the arrival of her father. The usual one-hour drive became an agonizing three hours of immense anticipation and apprehension. How does one break such heartbreaking news to a single father who had dedicated his life to raising his daughter with love, protection, and care? How could she confess that, at only thirteen years old, she had engaged in such inappropriate behavior?

Finally, the father arrived, wearied by the prolonged journey. Little did he know that this day would mark the moment his world would crumble around him. He entered the room, his face mirroring the exhaustion and concern that had plagued him throughout the seemingly endless drive. As she looked at her father, her heart ached for the pain she knew would befall him.

Together, her support system guided the devastated father through the unimaginable. They reassured him that this incident did not define his daughter's worth or their family's values. They explained that mistakes happened, even in the most protective environments, and how they handled them truly mattered. The journey towards healing and redemption began as they sought the professional help they desperately needed, surrounded themselves with understanding individuals, and made the difficult decision to change their daughter's environment for a fresh start.

Days she turned into weeks and weeks into months. The young girl began to find solace in her newfound support system. Love, patience, and understanding became the cornerstones of her recovery. Alongside therapy sessions and a newfound sense of purpose, she started to heal the wounds that had scarred her deeply. Though the road to redemption was arduous, her determination to rewrite her narrative fueled her every step.

As she journeyed through high school, she refused to let her past define her. Instead, she utilized the lessons learned from her mistakes as stepping stones toward personal growth. She worked diligently, pouring her heart and soul into her studies, determined to exceed expectations and prove that her journey did not define her capabilities.

On graduation day, she arrived, an emotional milestone in her battle for redemption. With tears of pride and joy in her father's eyes, she walked across the stage, collecting her diploma as an exemplary student. The applause that filled the auditorium was not merely for academic achievements but a celebration of her resilience, determination, and unwavering spirit. College beckoned, a new chapter in her life unfolding. Armed with the knowledge that mistakes do not define one's worth, she embraced the opportunity with open arms. She excelled in her studies, engaging in campus activities and fostering relationships built on trust and compassion.

She became an advocate, sharing her story with others who had experienced similar hardships, breaking the cycle of secrecy and shame. Her words became a lifeline for those trapped by their past, offering hope that healing and redemption were possible. Her journey had transformed her, not only as an individual but also as a beacon in the lives of others. She stood as a testament to the resilience of the human spirit, proving that mistakes were not insurmountable obstacles but opportunities for growth and transformation.

Her story became an anthem of hope, resonating with countless individuals who sought solace and a chance at a new beginning. Through her perseverance, she rebuilt her life and ignited a flame of possibility in the hearts of others. In the end, her story served as a reminder that no matter how deep the darkness may seem, light always has the potential to break through. Redemption was not a distant dream but a tangible reality, waiting to be embraced by those who dared to believe in its transformative power.

7: The Power of Connection: A Teacher's Journey from Detachment to Transformation

T he adage, "People don't learn from people they don't like," echoed in the minds of educators. It was a sentiment that many believed that to truly reach and inspire students, a teacher had to connect with them. However, one teacher vehemently disagreed with this notion - Ms. Stubbs.

To her, teaching was simply a duty, not a popularity contest. She firmly believed that her role was to impart knowledge, and that the student was responsible for learning. And so, year after year, she approached her job with an iron-clad determination to teach, disregarding any desire to be liked.

Ms. Stubbs was known throughout the school for her meticulous lesson plans, meticulously created charts, and meticulously prepared PowerPoint presentations. Her dedication to teaching was unquestionable - she was never late for school, rarely missed a day, and always seemed in control. Yet, despite her efforts, there was a lingering mystery as to why her students consistently failed to achieve good results, regardless of the grade level she taught. It was time to delve deeper into the heart of her teaching practice.

Over several months, I decided to observe Ms. Stubbs in action closely. I discovered a teacher devoid of human connection, a machine running on autopilot. An unmistakable air of coldness and aloofness emanated from her, leaving her students feeling unimportant and misunderstood. It was no wonder that they struggled to find motivation in her class. She seemed to harbor a deep-seated resentment toward her students, and this disdain was reflected in her rigid demeanor.

Finally, I mustered the courage to approach Ms. Stubbs and share my observations. It was met with staunch denial as if she was being unfairly judged. She pointed fingers at her students, blaming their attitudes towards school for their lack of progress. She clearly viewed teaching as a one-way street, where knowledge was imparted without considering the students' emotional well-being or engagement.

However, I couldn't accept this defeatist attitude towards education. Teaching was meant to be a relational journey where educators formed positive connections with their students to impact their lives positively. I understood that Ms. Stubbs had all the necessary tools and resources to be an exceptional teacher. Still, she was missing one crucial prerequisite—the ability to build meaningful relationships with her students.

To support her growth as an educator, I proposed a mentoring program to improve her relational skills. I explained that it was not about winning popularity contests or indulging her students but about creating an environment where trust, understanding, and empathy thrived. Despite her initial resistance, she eventually agreed to participate, perhaps out of a genuine desire to see improvement in her students.

The journey towards transformation began with introspection. Ms. Stubbs had to confront her own beliefs and biases, acknowledging that her approach had been flawed. Through extensive discussions and guided reflections, she started unraveling the layers of detachment that had surrounded her for many years. It was not an easy process; it required her to confront her insecurities and fears, but she bravely persevered.

Slowly but surely, Ms. Stubbs began to open her heart and mind to her students. She learned the power of truly listening to understand their struggles, hopes, and dreams. She discovered that a kind word, a genuine smile, or a compassionate gesture could uplift and inspire her students in ways she never anticipated. The coldness that had once defined her demeanor began to thaw, revealing a newfound warmth and empathy.

Soon, Ms. Stubbs started to embrace creativity and innovation in her teaching methods. No longer relying solely on rigid lesson plans and impersonal PowerPoint presentations, she incorporated interactive activities, group discussions, and real-world connections into her lessons. This shift ignited a spark within her students as they began to see the knowledge's relevance and applicability.

As the months passed, the classroom dynamic underwent a dramatic transformation. Students who had once disengaged or rebelled against the monotony of Ms. Stubbs' teaching methods now eagerly participated in class discussions. Their academic progress started to soar as their confidence and motivation grew. It was evident that the power of connection was a catalyst for change, not only in Ms. Stubbs but in each student she touched.

Ms. Stubbs' personal growth was undeniable. In her eyes, I witnessed a newfound sense of purpose and fulfillment. No longer simply going through the motions of teaching, she had discovered the true joy of educating young minds. Her dedication remained unwavering, but now it was fueled by a genuine passion for making a difference in the lives of her students.

The impact extended beyond the classroom walls. As word spread about Ms. Stubbs' transformation, fellow teachers began seeking her guidance. A ripple effect was created as educators across the school prioritized building relationships and connecting with their students. The notion that learning was a collaborative endeavor rather than a one-sided transaction became ingrained in the school culture.

In the end, Ms. Stubbs became a beacon of hope and inspiration. Her journey served as a testament to the transformative power of human connection within education. It proved that teaching was about imparting knowledge and creating an environment where students felt seen, heard, and valued.

"The Power of Connection: A Teacher's Journey from Detachment to Transformation" captured the essence of her remarkable evolution and reminded us of the profound impact that genuine relationships can have on shaping the lives and futures of our students. Ms. Stubbs taught us that teaching is not enough; we must also connect. By fostering an environment of trust, empathy, and understanding, we can unlock the potential within each student, empowering them to become lifelong learners and compassionate individuals.

"Let your ears be doorways to empathy, not avenues for judgment, and watch as deep connections and meaningful insights flow effortlessly."

8: From Devastation to Unity: Leading Through Tragedy

In a single moment, my entire career was shattered. It was a day like any other until I received a phone call that would change everything. As I sat in a seminar, surrounded by fellow educators on World Teachers Day, my phone buzzed incessantly. Sensing an emergency, I excused myself from the room, only to be met with devastating news. A student had been stabbed and killed on our campus by another student. I was filled with disbelief and an overwhelming sense of responsibility. Little did I know that this tragic event would become an opportunity for growth, unity, and creating a safer future for our school community.

The Moment of Truth. Upon receiving the news, my heart sank. I rushed to the hospital, desperate to see it for myself. As I entered the room and gazed upon the lifeless body of the student, I was struck by the absence of blood. How could such a simple accident result in such a devastating loss? Questions swirled in my mind as I grappled with the weight of this tragedy. My duty was to lead and guide our school through the darkest times. Tearfully, I questioned, "Why did God allow this to happen?" But there was no time for self-pity; I had to gather my strength and return to campus to face the challenge ahead.

Leading Through Chaos and Adversity. As I drove back to campus, my mind raced with a whirlwind of emotions. Our once vibrant hallways were filled with over 1200 grieving students, terrified and confused. Parents arrived in droves to collect their children, adding to the chaos. Word had spread rapidly, reaching the media, the police, and the education ministry. Meeting the gaze of devastated parents, I knew the most challenging part lay before me. Delivering the news of their child's untimely demise was a painful task. How could a place meant for growth and learning become a scene of tragedy? Yet, amidst the sorrow, the community rallied around us, entrusting their faith in my leadership.

A Foundation of Support. Tragedy has the power to bring people together like nothing else. We found solace in the community's unwavering support in our lowest moments. Counselors from all corners of the country flocked to our school, providing much-needed comfort and guidance to staff, students, and parents alike. It was awe-inspiring to witness the strength that emerges from unity. Gratitude fills my heart as I look back on all the hands extended to help us shoulder the weight of our grief.

We were turning Tragedy into Opportunity. Although the pain was unbearable, it also presented an opportunity for growth. We embarked on a healing journey, training our staff, revising policies, implementing new strategies, and acquiring better security equipment to minimize the risk of such a tragedy reoccurring. Weeks turned into a flurry of media interviews, regular sessions with parents, and navigating through legal matters. In the face of adversity, we stood firm, anchored in our unwavering honesty and sincerity. These actions built a bridge of trust with the parents who had lost their beloved children. We grieved together, knowing that our commitment as educators was to create a safe space for their children, molding them into responsible individuals striving for a better society.

Reflecting on our journey from devastation to unity, I am filled with a profound sense of purpose. The tragedy that threatened to consume us brought us closer as a community. We learned valuable lessons, converted pain into action, and planted seeds for a safer future. While the weight of leadership in education can be heavy, mainly when guiding children from fractured societies, our unwavering commitment to creating safe schools and fostering responsible, empathetic individuals makes it worthwhile.

Through this harrowing experience, we were reminded of our innate resilience and our determination to build a society that cherishes and nurtures the potential of every student. "From Devastation to Unity: Leading Through Tragedy to Create a Safer Future" is a testament to the strength of the human spirit and a call to action for all educators and leaders to prioritize the safety and well-being of those in their care.

9: Beyond the Classroom

To be a different type of leader who listens and stands by their word. These thoughts echoed through my mind as I walked through the school gates. The atmosphere was tense, a palpable unease that seemed to coat every surface. The news had spread like wildfire - there was a report that Tommy, one of our students, had brought a gun to school.

Tommy, a quiet and respectful student who rarely spoke, was an enigma to his classmates and teachers. He maintained

reasonable grades and never got into trouble. Yet, here we were, faced with the shocking possibility that he could be involved in such a dangerous act.

As I walked towards the school entrance, I could see the presence of authority gathering - the police and the teachers, all there to unravel the truth behind the allegation. But amidst the chaos and confusion, one person stood out from the crowd. Tommy patiently awaited me, his eyes scanning the sea of concerned faces, searching for a glimmer of trust.

At that moment, my heart sank. It dawned on me that Tommy believed I was the only one he could confide in and who would truly listen. This realization carried with it the weight of responsibility. I had to be that leader; he desperately needed someone who would not only listen but also stand by their word, offering him the support and help he so desperately required.

Taking a deep breath, I approached Tommy and assured him I would do everything I could to ensure he received the help and support he needed. His eyes softened, and a faint smile graced his lips. Tommy took my outstretched hand, and together, we walked towards the bathroom where the gun had been hidden, wrapped in a plastic bag, and immersed into the toilet tank.

As we entered the bathroom, a surreal stillness settled over us. We seemed to stand still as Tommy directed my gaze towards the concealed weapon. I couldn't help but feel a mix of relief and apprehension. We had found the gun and averted a potential disaster, but what would come next?

With a sense of cautious determination, I carefully retrieved the weapon from its hiding place, ensuring it was secured. I felt a surge of confidence as I clutched the bag, knowing that we had won a battle. But little did I know that the war was far from over.

Walking into the principal's office, I expected to be greeted with appreciation and gratitude for my role in diffusing the situation. To my surprise, however, the atmosphere was tense and unhappy. The principal's face was etched with a pained expression, and I struggled to comprehend what was happening.

I was then instructed to leave, to remove myself from the situation entirely. The confusion and disbelief washed over me in waves. How could this be? What was happening to Tommy? It was only later that I discovered the harsh truth. It had been determined that Tommy had stumbled upon the gun on his way to school. He had taken it not out of malice or ill intent but out of curiosity. The act that had initially seemed so ominous was now revealed to be nothing more than a misguided moment of intrigue.

I couldn't help but feel a sense of betrayal. Tommy, a boy who had placed his trust in me, had been failed by the system meant to protect and guide him. He had been labeled a threat, expelled from the school, and taken into custody. At that moment, I vowed to myself that I would do whatever it took to ensure that no other student would face a similar fate.

That year, as I continued my work as an educator, the story of Tommy lingered in my mind like a haunting melody. It became my driving force, my motivation to strive for change. I knew that I needed to become a principal and take on a leadership role that would allow me to shape and mold the educational system in a way that would support and uplift students like Tommy.

With unwavering determination, I embarked on a journey to acquire the necessary skills and knowledge to make a lasting impact. I pursued higher education, immersing myself in the study of educational leadership, psychology, and child development. I sought out mentors who shared my vision and actively sought opportunities to engage with like-minded individuals who were equally passionate about transforming the lives of young people.

Through my studies and experiences, I began to uncover the inherent flaws within the educational system. I realized that it was not enough to teach subjects and impart knowledge. Education had to be about fostering empathy, nurturing resilience, and instilling a sense of purpose in every student.

Armed with this newfound understanding, I embarked on my journey as a principal. My priority was to create an environment where students felt safe, supported, and understood. I implemented programs and initiatives focused on building relationships, encouraging open dialogue, and promoting emotional well-being.

Gone were the days of passively observing from the sidelines. I actively sought opportunities to connect with my students and listen to their hopes, fears, and aspirations. I created spaces within the school where they felt comfortable sharing their thoughts, knowing their voices would be heard, valued, and respected.

One of these spaces was the creation of a student-led council. This council, consisting of representatives from each grade level, served as a platform for students to participate actively in the decision-making process. They were given a voice and a sense of ownership over their educational experience, proving instrumental in shaping school policies and initiatives.

But it wasn't just about empowering the students. I also recognized the importance of cultivating a strong community among the faculty and staff. By fostering a culture of collaboration and support, I ensured that all school community members felt valued and appreciated. I encouraged professional development opportunities, provided resources and training, and promoted a sense of shared purpose and collective responsibility.

As the years passed, the impact of my leadership style became increasingly evident. Students thrived, not only academically but also emotionally and socially. They developed a deep sense of empathy and compassion, supporting and uplifting one another in need. Bullying incidents drastically decreased, replaced by a sense of unity and acceptance.

One particular incident stands out in my memory, serving as a testament to the transformative power of trust and compassion. A troubled student named Sarah approached me one day, her eyes filled with fear and desperation. She confided in me that she had been a victim of domestic abuse, enduring unspeakable horrors at the hands of her own family.

My heart broke for Sarah, and I knew I had to intervene. With the utmost sensitivity and confidentiality, I connected her with the appropriate resources and support systems. We developed a safety plan, empowering her to take control of her life and break free from the chains that bound her.

The journey was far from easy, but with a network of support and compassion, Sarah emerged as a survivor, resilient and determined. Witnessing the transformation within her filled me with an indescribable sense of pride and conviction. It solidified my belief that education was about imparting knowledge and empowering individuals to overcome adversity and build lives of value and purpose.

As the years rolled on, Tommy's story began to fade into the background, no longer a constant reminder of my failures but a catalyst for change. The impact of my leadership extended far beyond the confines of the school walls. I actively advocated for educational reform, addressing the systemic issues perpetuating the cycle of failure and despair.

I connected with educators nationwide through advocacy, sharing stories, strategies, and insights. We challenged the status quo, questioning outdated practices and demanding a shift towards a more holistic and inclusive educational experience. Together, we persisted, fueled by a shared belief in the transformative power of education.

I received a letter that warmed my heart during one of these advocacy conferences. It was from Tommy, now a young adult serving in the military. He thanked me for my impact on his life and expressed gratitude for the support I had extended him all those years ago. He found peace and purpose, serving his country honorably and with dedication.

When I read Tommy's words, tears filled my eyes. At that moment, I realized the profound effect educators can have on the lives of their students. We have the unique privilege and responsibility to shape minds, nurture souls, and ignite a spark of potential within each student.

In a harsh and unforgiving world, we must forge citizens of value who will positively impact the world. We must be the leaders who listen, stand by our word, and instill a sense of purpose and compassion in our students. Only then can we transform education and build a better future for all.

10: Student Discipline Redefined

Sandra, a vibrant grade 8 student, radiated positivity and a zest for life. However, one aspect of her behavior seemed to hinder her progress consistently—she was always late for school. As the Dean of Discipline, I ensured that all students adhered to the rules and faced appropriate consequences for their actions. In Sandra's case, it was time for her to face detention and community service due to her chronic tardiness.

However, reflecting on discipline and its true purpose, I realized that it extended beyond simply punishing students for their mistakes. Proper discipline required a comprehensive understanding between all parties involved, especially for those who were being disciplined. It was essential to delve deeper into the reasoning behind their actions to grasp the underlying challenges they may be facing.

With this perspective in mind, I decided to approach detention differently. Instead of blindly enforcing the rules, I dedicated 10- 15 minutes to having a conversation with each student, including Sandra. Little did I know that the conversation that ensued with Sandra would be more enlightening than I could have ever imagined.

Sandra's eyes sparkled with apprehension and anticipation as we talked. She began to open up, sharing a part of her life that remained hidden from the school community until now. It turned out that Sandra's life was a balancing act, one in which she displayed far more discipline than we could have ever fathomed.

Sandra shared that every morning, well before the crack of dawn, she assumed her role as the CEO, operations manager, and laborer of a small farm in her backyard. It was a farm that sustained both her and her bedridden grandmother, who served as her sole guardian. Raising chickens and pigs became their only source of income, their lifeline in adversity.

"My grandma is all I have," Sandra explained, her voice filled with resilience. "We lost my parents a few years ago, and it's just been the two of us ever since. The farm is my way of caring for her and ensuring we have enough to survive."

At that moment, a wave of realization washed over me. Sandra's delay was not a result of negligence or a lack of discipline. It was a consequence of circumstances beyond her control. She made a tremendous sacrifice each day by prioritizing her farm responsibilities before even considering attending school.

Driven to comprehend the gravity of Sandra's situation, I felt compelled to visit her home and meet her grandmother. The experience was eye-opening. Walking into their modest abode, I saw the resilience and determination emanating from Sandra and her grandmother. Despite the challenges, they exuded warmth, strength, and a profound love for one another.

In that moment, witnessing firsthand the reality of Sandra's life, the guidance counselor and I realized the support we could offer. It was clear that Sandra possessed incredible entrepreneurial skills that deserved nurturing and guidance. We decided to purchase chickens from her farm for the school canteen, contingent upon her maintaining good grades. This gesture acknowledged Sandra's hard work and dedication and provided her with a sense of empowerment and achievement.

We also connected Sandra with local farming organizations, providing her with resources, mentorship, and growth opportunities. Through these partnerships, Sandra expanded her knowledge, learned new farming techniques, and further enhanced her entrepreneurial prowess. It was an investment not only in Sandra's future but in her entire community as she began to share her newfound expertise with others in need.

As Sandra's academic performance improved and her responsibilities on the farm remained intact, we saw her blossom into a confident and ambitious young woman. With each passing day, she epitomized the values of discipline, resilience, and determination. Our support did more than alleviate her financial burdens; it instilled in her a belief in her capabilities and potential.

The impact of Sandra's story rippled throughout the school community. It served as a humbling reminder that, sometimes, discipline goes beyond strict adherence to rules. It requires the willingness to listen, empathize, and extend a helping hand to those who need it most. It forced us to question our preconceived notions and judgments, leading us to recognize the importance of equity and the pursuit of justice.

As a result of Sandra's experience, we implemented changes within the school system to accommodate better students facing similar challenges. We developed a mentorship program that allowed students to engage with professionals in various fields, exposing them to potential career opportunities and expanding their horizons. We also established a scholarship fund for students who showcased exceptional dedication and resilience in the face of adversity, ensuring that financial barriers would never hinder their pursuit of education.

Looking back on Sandra's journey, I realize that her story is not just about discipline or entrepreneurship; it transcends those boundaries. It is a testament to the power of compassion, empathy, and genuine understanding. It is a reminder that the most extraordinary individuals and stories can sometimes be found in ordinary places.

Today, Sandra has grown into a strong and accomplished woman. She has successfully expanded her farm, offering employment opportunities to others within her community. She inspires her peers by motivating them to identify their own strengths, embrace their challenges, and cultivate resilience.

As educators, we firmly believe that our duty extends beyond simply imparting knowledge. It is our responsibility to uplift, support, and guide our students, molding them into compassionate and empathetic individuals who will positively impact the world. Sandra's story is a constant reminder of the transformative power of listening, understanding, and offering support to those who need it most. It is a reminder that by doing so, we can cultivate a generation of individuals who are not defined by their circumstances but rather their ability to rise above them.

11: Parallel Realities

In the halls of Barks High School, Sandy's reputation shone bright like a star, a beacon of excellence and leadership. She stood tall, her grades were a testament to her dedication, and her leadership symbolized her influence. But beneath the facade of success lurked a hidden pain, a darkness threatening to consume her.

On that fateful morning, Sandy's world shattered like glass, her composure cracking under the weight of unspeakable trauma. As Mr. Brown's hand brushed her back in a familiar gesture, the floodgates of suppressed agony burst open, unleashing a fury born of years of silent suffering.

In the aftermath of the chaos, a harrowing truth emerged as the dust settled and sanity returned. Sandy's tormentor was not a shadowy stranger but a figure close, trusted, and vile. Her stepfather's deplorable actions mirrored Mr. Brown's innocent touch, blurring the lines between safety and danger, care and abuse.

As the adults grappled with the implications of Sandy's outburst, a stark choice loomed before them. Would they offer compassion, understanding, and support to a wounded soul in desperate need? Or would they turn their backs, succumbing to fear, ignorance, and prejudice?

In a cruel twist of fate, the institution that once celebrated Sandy's achievements now stood poised to deliver a crushing blow. Expulsion, the ultimate rejection, loomed large, a punishment that would only deepen her wounds and scar her soul.

But in the face of adversity, a glimmer of hope emerged a chance for redemption, healing, and transformation. What if the adults chose empathy, advocacy, and intervention instead of condemnation? What if they recognized Sandy's trauma as a call for help, not a cry for punishment?

In a parallel reality, a different path unfolds. The teachers, the counselor, and the principal united in a mission of compassion, rallying around Sandy and offering her the support she so desperately craves. Together, they create a safe space, a sanctuary of healing, where her pain is acknowledged, her voice is heard, and her spirit is nurtured.

As Sandy finds solace in the embrace of caring hearts, as she learns to trust, hope, and dream again, a new chapter begins. Her journey from darkness to light becomes a testament to resilience, the power of love, and the possibility of redemption.

And in this alternate ending, as Sandy's story unfolds, a question lingers in the air. What if we, too, were faced with a similar choice? What if, when confronted with a soul in need, we chose compassion over condemnation, empathy over judgment, love over fear?

In the end, Sandy's story is told alongside our own. The choices we make in moments of crisis and grace can shape not just one life but the world around us.

12: Look, Listen, the Signs are Always There...

In a small town where whispers echoed through the narrow streets, and secrets lurked behind closed doors, Suzan's childhood was shrouded in shadows that no one dared to shine a light upon. The first words out of her mother's mouth were not words of comfort or reassurance but a command, a demand to lie, to bury the truth deep within the silence of her soul.

Suzan, a fragile flower with petals tainted by the touch of her stepfather's cruel hands, lived a life of torment and despair. At the tender age of 9, innocence was ripped from her like petals torn from a rose, leaving behind a thorned stem piercing her heart each passing day. The world seemed to freeze, the colors fading to gray as she struggled to comprehend why a figure, she should have trusted had betrayed her most unspeakably. The memory of those violated boundaries haunted her waking hours and tormented her dreams at night.

As the years wore on, Suzan's spirit wilted like a neglected garden, her laughter fading into whispers of pain only she could hear. She retreated into herself, building invisible walls to protect the remnants of her shattered soul. The once vibrant and curious girl became a shell of who she once was, weighed down by shame and self-loathing. Each passing day felt like a test of endurance, a relentless battle with the demons that lingered within.

By the time she reached the age of 15, Suzan bore the weight of her suffering like a heavy cloak, suffocating her with each breath she took. The scars on her body told a tale of hidden agony, a language of despair etched into her skin by the blade she wielded in a desperate attempt to escape the prison of her mind. Each cut was a cry for help, a plea for someone to see beyond the façade of a girl who smiled but wept inside. But the world remained oblivious to her silent screams, imprisoned by ignorance and indifference.

Amid this darkness, a flicker of hope emerged. In the quiet solitude of her former teacher's office amidst shelves of dusty books and the soft hum of a distant classroom, Suzan's authentic voice found its courage to speak. With trembling lips and tear-stained cheeks, she unraveled the dark tapestry of her past, revealing the horror that had haunted her for so long.

Her teacher listened with a heart heavy with sorrow, a soul burdened by a child's suffering. With gentle hands and a kindly voice, she promised Suzan that she would not face this nightmare alone, that justice would be sought, and that healing would begin. The teacher's unwavering support became a lifeline for Suzan, reminding her that she was not defined by the trauma she had endured.

The wheels of fate turned swiftly as the relevant authorities were called into action, their voices a symphony of determination and resolve. Suzan was cloaked in a blanket of support, her trembling hands held steady by those who vowed to stand by her side to fight for her right to reclaim the stolen innocence of her youth.

In the aftermath of turmoil and tumult, Suzan emerged from the ashes of her pain like a phoenix rising from the flames. With a heart forged in the crucible of suffering, she vowed to dedicate her life to a cause greater than herself, to become a beacon of hope for those lost in the shadows of despair.

Through therapy and counseling, Suzan began to navigate the treacherous terrain of healing. It was a long and arduous journey, filled with moments of doubt and despair, but she refused to let her past define her future. With each step forward, she chipped away at the walls that had held her captive for so long, transforming them into stepping stones of resilience and strength.

And so, Suzan, once a victim of unspeakable cruelty, transformed into a warrior of compassion, a guardian angel for the wounded souls who tread the path she once walked alone. As a social worker, she cradled children's broken hearts in her arms, weaving a tapestry of love and healing that spanned the threads of time. Her presence was a balm for the wounded, a song of solace for the weary, a ray of light in the darkest night. With each smile she bestowed, each hand she held, she whispered a silent promise never to forget the child she once was, never to forsake the innocence that was stolen from her grasp.

In the tapestry of life, Suzan's story was a thread of resilience, a testament to the power of courage in the face of adversity. Through her pain, she found purpose; through her suffering, she found strength; through her tears, she found healing. And in the gentle echo of her laughter, in the warmth of her embrace, in the light of her unwavering spirit, Suzan became a living testament to the indomitable human spirit, a reminder that even in the darkest night, there shines a glimmer of hope, a beacon of light that guides the lost back home.

As the years passed, Suzan's work as a social worker touched the lives of countless children, giving them the chance to reclaim their own stolen innocence. She fought tirelessly to dismantle the walls of silence and shame that imprisoned them, standing as a voice for the voiceless and a pillar of strength for the broken. Her journey was not without struggles; healing is not a linear path. But with each child whose life she touched, she saw the ripple effect of her transformation, each small victory a testament to the resilience of the human spirit.

Though the scars of her past would never truly fade, Suzan wore them as badges of honor, reminders of her triumph over adversity. She became a beacon of light, illuminating the path for those lost in their darkness. Through her story, she dared to challenge society's reluctance to confront and address the uncomfortable truths hidden beneath the surface. She urged others to break free from the chains that held them captive, find strength in vulnerability, and embrace compassion's healing power.

Suzan's journey was a testament to the resilience of the human spirit, a reminder that hope can bloom even in the face of unspeakable horror. Her courageous pursuit of justice and healing catalyzed change, sparking conversations and igniting a movement that sought to eradicate the scourge of abuse from society's shadows.

In the end, Suzan's legacy was not defined by the darkness of her past but by the light she brought into the lives of others. Her unwavering dedication to making the world a better place, one child at a time, touched the hearts of those who knew her story. And as her name echoed through the halls of resilience and compassion, it served as a reminder that even in the face of unimaginable pain, the human spirit can transcend, transform, and ultimately triumph.

13: The Vision: The Transformed School

Once upon a time, in a small town nestled in the rolling hills of the countryside, there stood a school like no other. This was not just a place where children learned mathematics and history but a sanctuary where they could grow, be safe, be rescued, heal, and discover their best selves.

The school was like a second home to the children walking through its doors daily. With their kind smiles and gentle words, the teachers welcomed the students with open arms, ready to guide them on their educational journey. But this school was more than just a place of learning; it was a place of refuge for those who needed it most.

A young girl named Emily had recently transferred to the school. Her troubled past was filled with pain and uncertainty. She arrived with a heavy heart, unsure of what the future held. But she felt a sense of peace when she stepped foot in the school. The teachers quickly noticed the sadness in her eyes and took her under their wings, offering her a safe space to heal and grow.

One day, during art class, Emily sat quietly at her desk, staring blankly at the page before her. The teacher, Mr. Thompson, approached her with a kind smile and asked her what was wrong. Emily hesitated at first, unsure if she should open up to him. But something in his gentle eyes encouraged her to speak. "I just feel lost," she whispered, her voice barely above a whisper. "I don't know who I am or where I belong."

Mr. Thompson listened intently, his heart breaking for the young girl before him. He knew that Emily needed more than just academic guidance; she needed someone to help her discover her true self. So, he made it his mission to show her that she could do so much more than she realized. Over the coming weeks, Mr. Thompson worked closely with Emily, encouraging her to try new things and step out of her comfort zone. He noticed her talent for painting and encouraged her to express herself through art. As Emily's confidence grew, so did her sense of belonging. She began to see the school not just as a place of learning but as a place where she could truly be herself.

As the months passed, Emily blossomed into a bright, confident young woman. She no longer walked the halls with her head hung low, but her chin held high, a smile on her face. She had found her place in the school, where she could grow, be safe, and discover her best self. However, Emily was not the only student whose life was touched by the school. There was also a young boy named David, who had endured his struggles. He was quiet and reserved, always keeping to himself. But the teachers saw the spark of potential in him and knew that with the proper guidance, he could flourish.

One day, David's project went awry during a science experiment, causing a small explosion in the classroom. The other students laughed and pointed fingers, but the teacher, Miss Roberts, saw the fear and humiliation in David's eyes. She knew that he needed reassurance, not ridicule. After class, Miss Roberts pulled David aside and offered him a kind smile. "It's okay to make mistakes, David," she said softly. "That's how we learn and grow."

David's eyes widened in surprise. No one had ever spoken to him with such kindness before. He realized that the school was not just a place of judgment but of understanding and acceptance. From that moment on, David began to open up more, slowly breaking out of his shell.

Miss Roberts encouraged David to join the school's robotics club, knowing he had a knack for building and creating. And as David delved into the world of robotics, he discovered a passion he never knew he had. He poured his heart and soul into each project, his eyes lighting up with excitement. Before long, David had become the star of the robotics club, his creations winning awards and recognition. The other students looked up to him with admiration, and David finally felt like he belonged. The school had given him a second chance to grow, be rescued, and discover his best self.

As the years passed, Emily and David became shining examples of what the school stood for. They had both faced adversity and doubts, but with the support of their teachers and peers, they had overcome their obstacles and emerged more vital than ever. They had learned that the school was not just a place of academic pursuit but a place of love, encouragement, and growth.

And so, the small-town school continued to be a beacon of hope for all who walked through its doors. It was a place where children could be nurtured and supported, heal their wounds, and build a brighter future. It was a place where students could truly discover their best selves and take their place in the world with confidence and pride. As the sun set over the rolling hills of the countryside, casting a golden light over the school, the children knew they were truly home. They knew that in this place of learning and love, they would always find safety, comfort, and a guiding hand to lead them on their educational journey.

14: Unseen Potential: A Tale of Redemption

The classroom fell silent as the inspector's question hung in the air. The students, eager to impress, searched their minds for an answer. But their collective knowledge fell short, and a heavy atmosphere settled upon them. Among them, Adam, a young boy with unkempt hair and tattered clothes, raised his hand as high as he could, desperate for recognition. Yet, the education officer ignored him, rendering him invisible in the sea of faces.

As frustration bubbled within him, Adam could no longer contain himself. The words burst from his lips before he could think twice, the correct answer echoing through the room. However, instead of praise or admiration, the education officer's face twisted into a mask of anger. His voice thundered through the classroom, accusing Adam of insolence. "Shut up, you gutter rat!" he bellowed, the words burning into Adam's soul.

Adam, however, refused to allow the incident to break his spirit. He channeled his anger and humiliation into his studies, determined to prove himself despite the odds stacked against him. With his grandma as his only support, he sought solace in books and knowledge, finding a sanctuary from the harsh realities of his life.

As the years passed, Adam surpassed all expectations. After graduating from each stage of his education with remarkable honors, his intelligence and dedication shone brightly. His reputation as a diligent student reached the ears of prestigious universities, and they welcomed him with open arms. Now a renowned educator, Adam embarked on a journey to change the system that had once oppressed him.

With hard work and perseverance, Adam rose through the ranks of academia. He became a Superintendent, a leader in the field of education, and the supervisor of the very education officer who had once embarrassed him. The day arrived when they finally had a face-to-face meeting.

The education officer, oblivious to the connection between himself and Adam, fidgeted with anticipation, eager to impress the new Superintendent with tales of his achievements. He babbled on about his accomplishments, his voice filled with inflated self-importance. Now a PhD holder, Adam listened patiently, allowing the man to dig his shallow grave.

It was Adam's turn to introduce himself. As he looked into the eyes of the education officer, he spoke with a soft yet commanding voice that resonated through the room, his words carrying the weight of his journey. "I am that gutter rat," Adam announced, a simple sentence packed with years of hardship, determination, and triumph.

The education officer's face paled; his arrogance deflated in an instant. The realization of his past actions hit him like a tidal wave as he finally connected the dots between the young boy he once berated and the man standing before him now. Shame washed over him, and he fell silent, aware of the lesson life had just taught him.

The story's moral echoes through the corridors of our minds: Be careful how you treat others today, for they may become the architects of your redemption tomorrow. In a world where prejudices and judgments dictate our interactions, this tale serves as a reminder that true worth and potential lie within the depths of everyone, waiting to be nurtured and discovered.

It begs the question: How many geniuses, innovators, and dreamers have been silenced by others' unkindness? How many potential leaders, scientists, and artists have been lost because they could never prove themselves? Adam's story ignites a call to action, urging us to see beyond appearances, socio-economic backgrounds, and preconceived notions. It compels us to create a society that values the potential of every individual, regardless of where they come from or what they look like.

Let us remember that within the hearts and minds of those society deems as "gutter rats" are untold stories waiting to be written, souls yearning to soar, and dreams ready to be realized. And when we do, when we embrace the powerful journey of self-discovery and resilience, a world of infinite possibilities awaits us all.

15: Teacher Quality Matters

The Grade 4 class at Big Rock Primary School had earned a notorious reputation. They were known throughout the school for their unruly behavior and constant defiance of authority. No teacher wanted to be saddled with the responsibility of molding this seemingly unreachable bunch. The previous year, three teachers had resigned quickly, unable to handle the daily chaos and disobedience exhibited by the Grade 4 students. It was a definite challenge for the administrators to find a teacher who could tame this rowdy class and set them on the path to success

Then, amidst the frustration and uncertainty, arrived Ms. Allen. She was a teacher of exceptional caliber, known for her unwavering commitment to her students' success. Determined to make a difference in the lives of these seemingly lost individuals, she arrived at Big Rock Primary with a sense of purpose that outshined any other ordinary teacher. She refused to let the reputation of her new class deter her from her mission

Ms. Allen wasted no time in forging deliberate partnerships with the students' parents. Recognizing the importance of parental involvement, she reached out to every family in the class, ensuring that they were aware of her commitment and seeking their support in her efforts to transform their children's lives. She organized regular meetings, shared her plans, listened to their concerns, and devised strategies for collaboration. This level of involvement and transparency alone gave the parents renewed hope that their children were now in good hands

But that was just the start. Ms. Allen knew that she had to go beyond the confines of the classroom to impact her students truly. She began taking them on outings and educational excursions, exposing them to experiences they had never encountered. Whether it was a trip to a local museum, a nearby wildlife preserve, or even a live theatre performance, Ms. Allen wanted her students to see the world beyond the walls of their classroom. These excursions served multiple purposes - they sparked the students' curiosity, broadened their horizons, and offered them a glimpse into a different reality that awaited them beyond their current challenges

In addition to these eye-opening experiences, Ms. Allen created a structured environment within her classroom that was never broken, even in her absence. She understood that consistency was key to reshaping the behavior and mindset of her students. It was not an easy task, given the ingrained habits that had developed over the years. However, Ms. Allen's unwavering discipline, combined with her natural ability to connect with her students, slowly began to chip away at their resistance

She implemented a set of established rules and expectations that every student had to adhere to. She rewarded the students for displaying positive behavior, going out of her way to acknowledge their efforts and celebrate their achievements. This positive reinforcement soon became the driving force behind the students' desire to change, as they realized that their actions had a direct impact on their own lives and the overall atmosphere of the classroom.

The transformation was not immediate, nor was it without its fair share of setbacks. There were days when Ms. Allen questioned her own abilities and wondered if she was truly making a difference. It was during these challenging moments that she relied on her unwavering determination and unparalleled dedication to keep pushing forward. She reminded herself of the potential that lay dormant within each of her students, waiting to be unleashed. She believed in them, even when they failed to believe in themselves.

As the months passed, Ms. Allen's efforts began to yield remarkable results. The Grade 4 class, previously known for their renegade behavior, started to blossom into responsible and engaged learners. Their once chaotic classroom now buzzed with an electric energy as students eagerly participated in discussions, completed their assignments diligently, and demonstrated a thirst for knowledge they had never shown before.

Outside the classroom, their newfound enthusiasm spilled over into extracurricular activities. The Grade 4 class became the school's pride, representing Big Rock Primary in academic competitions, sports tournaments, and the arts. They were winning not only trophies and ribbons but also their peers' and teachers' admiration and respect. From being shunned as the class no one wanted to teach, they became the epitome of success and the embodiment of the transformative power of an exceptional educator.

The following year, as the Grade 4 students transitioned to Grade 5, they carried the lessons they had learned under Ms. Allen's guidance. Their academic performance soared to unprecedented heights, as they scored the highest average test scores the school had ever witnessed on a standardized exam. The administrators, who had once struggled to find a teacher willing to take on this seemingly unreachable bunch, now marveled at the astonishing progress made by these once-condemned students.

The impact of Ms. Allen's teaching extended far beyond the confines of the school. The success of the Grade 4 class soon became the talk of the town, attracting the attention of educators, parents, and policymakers alike. Media outlets highlighted the incredible journey of these students, showcasing the transformative potential of a dedicated teacher. Ms. Allen became a beacon of hope for educators across the nation, a shining example of how a single individual could make an indelible impact on the lives of their students.

Educational conferences and seminars were buzzing with discussions centered around Ms. Allen's teaching methods and strategies. Her approach, which focused on holistic development, parental involvement, and experiential learning, challenged traditional education norms. It sparked a renewed debate on the importance of teacher quality and provided a fresh perspective on tackling challenging and often neglected student populations.

In a world fixated on standardized test scores and academic achievement, Ms. Allen's success story was a wake-up call for educators and policymakers. It forced them to question their obsession with numbers and reminded them of the real purpose of education—to mold individuals who are not only academically proficient but also compassionate, curious, and well-rounded.

The impact was not limited to the educational realm alone. Parents started reevaluating their role in their children's education, realizing their involvement was crucial to their academic success. They began engaging in their children's learning journey, attending parent-teacher meetings, volunteering in the classroom, and becoming advocates for their children's education. This newfound synergy between parents and teachers fostered an environment where students thrived, surpassing expectations and breaking down the barriers that had previously held them back.

The story of the Grade 4 class at Big Rock Primary School symbolized hope and triumph, an embodiment of the infinite potential within every child, waiting to be unlocked. It served as a reminder that no child is beyond redemption, and no classroom is beyond saving. It was a testament to the power of teacher efficacy within an exceptional educator whose unwavering commitment and belief in her students shattered the chains of mediocrity and transformed a class once condemned into a collective force of success.

So, the next time someone tries to argue that teacher quality doesn't matter, let them hear the story of Ms. Allen and her Grade 4 class. Let them witness the awe-inspiring transformation within those classroom walls and see its profound impact on the lives of every individual involved. Let them understand that teachers can mold the future, one student at a time. And let them pause and rethink their assumptions, for in that pause lies the potential to truly revolutionize education and unleash the boundless possibilities within every child.